STARS AND GALAXIES

NECIA H. APFEL

FRANKLIN WATTS
NEW YORK / LONDON / TORONTO / SYDNEY / 1982
A FIRST BOOK

*FRONTIS: AN OPEN STAR CLUSTER IN
THE CONSTELLATION CANCER. THE
SIZE OF THE STAR IMAGES AS WELL AS
THE "POINTS" ON MANY OF THEM ARE
DUE TO THE LONG TIME EXPOSURE
AND PHOTOGRAPHIC PROCESS.*

Cover photograph of a globular cluster courtesy of
the U.S. Naval Observatory

Interior photographs courtesy of Palomar
Observatory, California Institute of Technology:
pp. 6, 25, 28 (Copyright by California Institute
of Technology, Palomar Observatory photograph),
32, 39 (bottom), 53 (top and bottom); Hansen
Planetarium: pp. 8, 10 (Naval Research Labora-
tory); U.S. Naval Observatory: pp. 26, 48;
Hale Observatories: p. 38; Lick Observatory:
pp. 39 (top), 45 (top), 47, 55; Necia Apfel:
p. 45 (bottom); *Odyssey* magazine: p. 63.

Diagram by Vantage Art

Library of Congress Cataloging in Publication Data

Apfel, Necia H.
Stars and galaxies.

(A First book)
Bibliography: p.
Includes index.
Summary: Discusses the formation, composition,
and placement of stars and groups of stars
throughout the universe.
1. Stars—Juvenile literature.   2. Galaxies—
Juvenile literature.   [1. Stars.   2. Galaxies]
I. Title.
QB801.7.A59   523.8   81-22011
ISBN 0-531-04389-4   AACR2

CONTENTS

STARS AND GALAXIES

CHAPTER ONE

WHAT IS A STAR?

Have you ever been out in the countryside on a clear, moonless night? If you have, you know how brilliant the stars appear in the sky. They seem almost countless.

People who lived long ago were much better acquainted with the stars than we are. They carefully counted all that they could see and knew where each one was in the sky. They noted how bright each one was and when it would be visible during the year. The brighter stars were given names so that they could be more easily identified.

Names were also given to groups of stars that appeared together in the sky and seemed to form a picture. These were the *constellations.* Usually these constellations were named after folk heroes, gods, or wild animals. Every early civilization throughout the world had its own set of constellations and its own folk stories about each one. The constellations we are most familiar with today are those from ancient Greece.

Since so many celestial objects are named after the constellations in which they are found, it is important that you become familiar with the constellations themselves and their locations in the sky. However, this is only the beginning of your

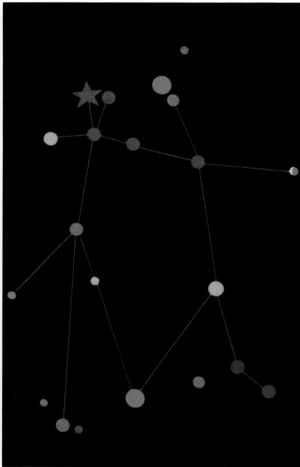

The Constellation Gemini, the Twins. In Greek mythology, this referred to Castor and Pollux, both athletic champions who were so devoted to one another that when Castor, the mortal twin, died, Pollux asked Zeus to take away his immortality and let him die also.

study. Those twinkling points of light in the night sky are more than mere beacons in the dark. But what are they?

A star is a ball of gas that shines very brightly. It is extremely big and extremely hot. The star closest to us is our own sun, which doesn't look like a star to us because it is so close in comparison to the other stars. Our sun is 93 million miles (about 150 million km) away. The next nearest star is 270,000 times farther away—about 25 trillion miles (40,000 billion km)!

Our star, the sun, has a diameter 109 times that of the earth. Over one million earths could fit into the sun. And yet the sun is a very average star. There are stars that are thousands of times larger. There are also stars that are as small as the earth.

All the stars that we see shining in the sky are very hot. The sun's surface temperature is about 10,000°F (5,550°C). The surface temperatures of other stars range from about 3,000°F (1,700°C) to over 60,000°F (33,000°C). Deep inside every star, the temperatures are even higher, tremendously higher in fact. The sun's central temperature, for example, is about 27 million degrees F (15 million degrees C).

Stars glow, or shine, because they are so big and so hot. They create their own energy. We see this energy in the form of starlight. We feel the heat of the sun's energy on a sunny day. Where does this energy come from?

The main ingredient in a star is the gas hydrogen. Hydrogen is the most abundant element in the universe. When atoms of hydrogen gas deep in the interior of a star are heated to millions of degrees and crushed under the enormous weight of the star, changes in their atomic structure take place. The hydrogen is changed into helium, which is the second most abundant element in the universe. This transformation from hydrogen to helium is called a *nuclear reaction*. Millions of such reactions take place in the center, or *core*, of a star every second. This is where the hydrogen atoms are most compact.

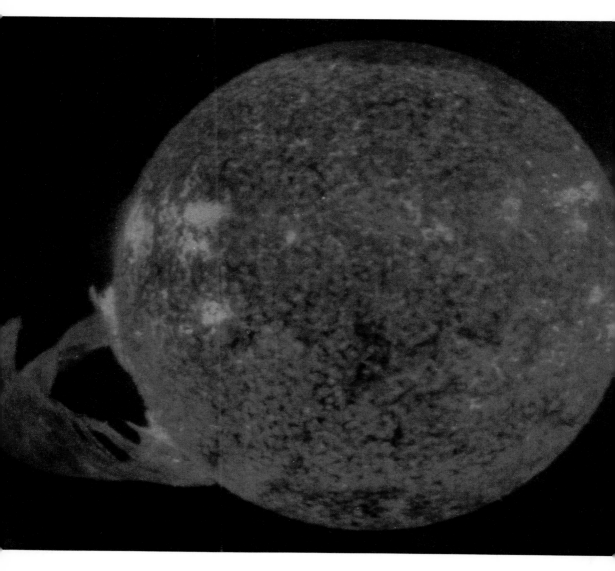

The sun, seen here during a solar eruption

Inside the core, it is like millions of hydrogen bombs all going off at once.

Not all the hydrogen is converted into helium, however. A very small part of it is changed into energy. This energy, created at the center of the star, pushes its way upward toward the surface. When it finally reaches the surface, it travels out into space and is seen as starlight.

Because hydrogen is continually being converted within the star into helium, new energy is constantly being created. This energy moves outward from the center of the star and pushes up against the layers of hot gases that are pushing down with their enormous weight. These two pressures offset each other, and the star remains stable and unchanging for a very long period of time.

This process has been going on deep inside of the sun for almost 5 billion years. Every second, over 600 million tons of hydrogen gas in the sun's core are transformed into 595 million tons of helium gas. The sun loses about 5 million tons of material every second; this is the amount that is converted into energy. Five million tons of matter may sound like a tremendous amount for the sun to lose, but in fact scientists believe that the sun still has enough hydrogen fuel to last for another 5 billion years.

CHAPTER TWO

HOW FAR ARE THE STARS?

The starlight we see is energy that was created from stellar material deep in the core of a star. This starlight has been traveling toward us for many years at the speed of light—about 186,300 (300,000 km) per second. Nothing travels faster than the speed of light.

Every year that the starlight travels through space it covers the distance of 1 light-year. A *light-year* is the distance that light travels in one year. Since the speed of light is 186,300 miles per second, 1 light-year is approximately 6 trillion miles (9,600 billion km). A string wrapped around the earth 236 million times would be about 1 light-year long.

Astronomers use the light-year as their yardstick instead of miles or kilometers because of the great distances they have to measure. Using miles to measure the distances to the stars would be like using inches to measure the distance between New York and San Francisco. For example, Alpha Centauri, the star nearest to the sun, is about 25 trillion miles (40,000 billion km) away. It is much easier to say that this star is 4⅓ light-years away.

Because light takes time to travel to us, the starlight we see today tells us how the star appeared when the light left it many years ago. It does not tell us anything about the star's present condition. For example, the light that we see from Alpha Centauri, which is 4⅓ light-years away, left that star 4⅓ years ago. How old were you then?

All the other stars are farther away, and therefore the light we see from them today is even older. Some stars are so far away that Columbus was just discovering America when their light started its long journey to us. Dinosaurs roamed the earth when the light from still more distant stars left them. There are even some stars so far away from us that their light began traveling toward the earth before the earth was even formed, some 4.6 billion years ago.

Distances to the stars vary greatly, but all are very far away as compared to anything here on earth. How do astronomers measure such enormous distances?

Hold one finger out at arm's length in front of your eyes. Now close one eye and note what object or objects the finger covers in the background. Open that eye and close the other. You will note that the finger appears to have shifted and now covers some other area. If you do this experiment in front of a bookcase, you can count the number of books the finger "shifted."

Now move your finger closer to your face and repeat the experiment. Is the "shift" larger or smaller? You will find that the closer you bring your finger to your face, the bigger the apparent shift will be.

Astronomers use this method, called *parallax,* to find distances to the nearest stars. The nearby star whose distance is being determined is the "finger" in the experiment. Much more distant stars provide the background against which the apparent shift can be measured.

Because of the huge distances involved, stellar shift

cannot be detected by simply opening and closing one's eyes. Instead, the opposite sides of the earth's orbit around the sun are used. Pictures of the star are taken six months apart, and these photographs serve as the "eyes" in the experiment. The shift of the nearby star against more distant stars is measured, just as the shift of your finger against a row of books could be measured. The greater the shift, the nearer the star. Astronomers measure the angles involved and by using mathematical formulas can compute the actual distances to the stars.

The apparent shift of your finger in the experiment was quite noticeable, but the parallactic shift of even nearby stars is extremely small. It cannot be detected without a telescope and some very precise measuring instruments.

Even the most precise and accurate measuring instruments, however, cannot detect the parallax of a star more than 300 light-years away. The shift in position is too small. Other methods must be used. However, all of these other methods depend upon the accuracy of the parallax measurements of nearby stars. If these measurements are in error, so are our estimates of the distances to the far reaches of the universe.

CHAPTER THREE

STARLIGHT...
STAR BRIGHT

Although people long ago did not realize how far away the stars were, they were very aware of the differences in brightness, and they kept careful records of these differences. The brightest stars were given names, many of which we still use today, although astronomers now have other systems for identifying stars.

One early method was to call the brightest star in each constellation "alpha," which is the first letter of the Greek alphabet. The second brightest star in the constellation was called "beta," and so forth. The name of the constellation was added to these Greek letters. This is one of many ways in which the Greek alphabet is still used in astronomy today.

Before the telescope was invented, this method of identifying stars was satisfactory. Only a few thousand stars are visible to the naked eye. However, in 1610, the famous Italian scientist Galileo Galilei turned the newly invented telescope toward the sky. He was amazed to find thousands upon thousands of stars that scientists of his day had never dreamed existed.

Later, as telescopes grew in size and power, the number of stars that were visible became overwhelming. The 200-inch (500-cm) telescope on Mt. Palomar in California can pick up the light of many billions of stars. Obviously, there were too many stars in each constellation to continue using the Greek alphabet for stellar identification.

New methods were introduced. Stars were given numbers based upon their location in the sky. Huge catalogs were printed giving the position, degree of brightness, and other information about each numbered star. Thousands of stars were thus identified. Yet even today less than 1 percent of all the stars in our galaxy have been cataloged. Instead, detailed photographs have been taken of each area of the sky, and faint, unnamed, and unnumbered stars are identified only by their position in relation to brighter stars nearby.

A star's brightness is, therefore, one very important way of describing it. But how do we measure brightness? In the second century B.C., the Greek astronomer Hipparchus decided that the stars could be conveniently grouped according to their level of brightness, or *magnitude.* He called the very brightest ones "first magnitude stars." The faintest stars that he could see were classified as "sixth magnitude stars."

Astronomers still use this magnitude system today, even with stars that are too dim to be seen without a telescope. The magnitude scale was simply extended beyond the sixth magnitude. For example, the telescope on Mt. Palomar can detect stars of the twenty-third magnitude. These stars appear more than a billion times fainter than the first magnitude stars.

When more precise measurements of the brightest stars were made, it was found that some were even brighter than the first magnitude. So the magnitude scale was extended in the other direction as well. A few stars have zero and minus magnitudes. The scale can also be applied to planets and other celestial objects.

Magnitude measurements are based upon how the star (or other celestial body) appears to us here on earth. But we know that the stars are not all the same distance from us. Their brightness may be due to their closeness to us or it may be due to their *real* luminosity, that is, the amount of actual light they give off. A nearby flashlight beam will appear brighter to us than a roaring campfire a mile (1.6 km) away.

The magnitudes we have been speaking of are called *apparent magnitudes* because they are measures of how bright the stars appear to us. In order to compare the real luminosities of the stars with each other, we would have to look at them all from the same distance away.

Of course, we cannot actually do this, and we know that distances to the stars vary greatly. However, astronomers have been able to calculate how bright each star would appear to us if they all really were at the same distance. Under such conditions we would quickly see that the roaring campfire was much brighter than the flashlight. This measure of brightness is called the star's *absolute magnitude.* It is how bright a star would appear to us if it were at the specific distance used in the calculations. In this way, if all the stars are compared, we can tell which ones are really the most luminous.

The same scale that is used for apparent magnitude is also used for absolute magnitude, but very few, if any, stars have the same magnitude on both scales. The sun, for example, has an absolute magnitude of only +4.8. If it were not so close to us, we would see it in the sky as just another relatively dim star. Other stars, on the other hand, are really much brighter than they appear to us, but because they are so very far away, they appear very dim.

Using the lists of the brightest and the nearest stars that you will find in the back of this book, you can compare absolute and apparent magnitudes. Remember that the lower the magnitude number, the brighter the star.

If we could group the stars according to their absolute magnitudes, they would form a sort of pyramid. At the very top would be a few extremely bright stars with absolute magnitudes of -7. For each of these stars we would find many thousands of less bright stars in the lower portion of the pyramid. The very faintest stars that we could detect with powerful telescopes have absolute magnitudes of about $+19$. Of course, there may be even fainter stars that we cannot see. We would find the sun at about midpoint in this pyramid of brightness. However, because there are so many more faint stars than bright ones, there are many more stars below the sun in the pyramid than there are above it.

If you compare the list of brightest stars with that of the nearest stars, you will find very few of the same stars listed in both groups. Although the bright stars are much fewer in number and are scattered much more widely throughout the galaxy, their brilliance enables us to see them at great distances.

CHAPTER FOUR

HOT STARS...
HOTTER STARS

All stars are very hot, but stellar temperatures vary widely. The surface temperature of a star is a very important clue as to what kind of star it is.

If two stars have the same surface temperature and are at the same distance from us, the larger star will be the brighter one. To understand this better, let us imagine a single candle burning some distance away from us. It will represent the smaller star. Nearby, at the same distance from us, a cluster of 1,000 identical candles is also burning. The cluster represents a much larger star (1,000 times larger) with the same surface temperature. The cluster of candles will be far brighter. It will give off more luminosity even though each of its candles gives off only as much light as the single candle does. Similarly, although a very powerful spotlight may be smaller in diameter than the 1,000-candle cluster, it may be far brighter because it has a higher surface temperature.

The same is true with stars. We must know the star's surface temperature in order to determine its size.

Light from any source can be thought of as a series of waves, like the waves on the surface of the ocean. Some ocean waves are small and come in rapid succession. Others are much larger and come less frequently. Light waves behave in the same way. The more frequent the light wave, the smaller it is. Longer light waves come less frequently. When the light hits our eyes, our brain interprets the wavelength and frequency of the light in terms of color. We see the color red when longer light waves enter our eyes and the color blue-violet when shorter ones are present. In between the red and blue-violet extremes are all the colors of the rainbow. One color fades into the next as the wavelength changes.

Light from a very hot source, such as the sun, is called *white light.* It is a mixture of many different wavelengths or colors all combined together. However, we can break up this white light by allowing it to pass through a prism. A prism is a thick piece of glass usually triangular in shape. The light is bent by the prism and separated into all of its various colors. We call these colors the light's *spectrum.*

Astronomers can photograph a star's spectrum by attaching a *spectrograph* to their telescopes. This special instrument combines a prism (or other light-dispersing device) with a camera. The photograph of a star's spectrum is called a *spectrogram.* It shows the spectrum of visible light received from the star. Each point on the spectrogram represents a specific wavelength of light.

Close examination of a spectrogram shows that there are many dark lines cutting through it. These are *spectral lines.* They are places in the spectrum of a star where the light has been absorbed by certain chemical elements in the star's atmosphere. Each element has its own characteristic set of spectral lines, which serve as a kind of chemical "fingerprint." By studying the positions of these spectral lines, astronomers can tell what elements are present in the star.

Hydrogen is the most abundant element in nearly all the stars. Helium is the next most abundant element. Most stars,

PRINCIPAL TYPE OF STELLAR SPECTRA

TYPE		STAR
O6		λ CEPHEI
B3		η AURIGAE
A0		δ CYGNI
F2		β CASSIOPEIA
G2		η PEGASI
K5		γ DRACONIS
M5		α HERCULIS
N0		19 PISCIUM
Se		R GEMINORUM

Examples of the principal types of stellar spectra

including the sun, have about 75 to 95 percent hydrogen and about 3 to 23 percent helium. The fraction remaining is composed of other elements, including carbon, oxygen, and iron.

However, not all stellar spectra (pl. of *spectrum*) look alike. Some have only a few broad lines while others have dozens of thin lines scattered over the entire spectrum. If most of the stars are similar in composition, what causes the differences in their spectra?

The differences are caused by variations in the surface temperatures of the stars. The spectral lines of each element appear most prominently at certain temperatures and may not be visible at all at other temperatures. Hydrogen spectral lines, for example, are prominent in the spectra of very hot stars but are faint or invisible in the spectra of cooler stars.

Many stellar spectra have been obtained and analyzed and the stars classified according to their surface temperatures. Letters of the alphabet were used to identify each spectral class. Originally, the classes followed normal alphabetical order, but later discoveries required that this order be rearranged. Now, from the highest surface temperatures to the lowest, the classes read: O, B, A, F, G, K, M.* The O-type stars have the hottest surface temperatures. M-type stars are the coolest.

Each stellar class was further divided into tenths, designated by the numbers 0 to 9. (Within each class, the lower the number, the hotter the star.) The reason for the further division was that differences between the classes were found to be gradual rather than sharp or distinct. Thus, stars are classified as A5, F8, K4, and so on. The sun is a G2 star.

We usually associate the color red with something hot. We speak of a very hot object as being "red-hot." However, if we

---

* Astronomy students have long used the following to learn this sequence: Oh, Be A Fine Girl; Kiss Me.

could continue to heat an object beyond the point at which it is red-hot, we would find that the redness gradually changes into orange, then yellow, and finally a blue-white glow.

This is true for stars as well. The coolest M-type stars have surface temperatures of about 6,000°F (3,300°C) and are red in color. The very hottest O-type stars are blue-white and have surface temperatures of more than 60,000°F (33,000°C. In between these extremes we find orange and yellow stars. Our sun is a yellow star with a surface temperature of about 10,000°F (5,500°C).

As you can see from the star lists at the end of this book, some K- and M-type stars have much greater luminosities than others. If their surface temperatures are the same as the dimmer stars, then the brighter stars must be much bigger. They are like the cluster of candles compared to the single candle shining alone. We call such stars *giants* and *super-giants.*

CHAPTER FIVE

THE BIRTH OF A STAR

Why are some stars very large and others quite small in comparison? To answer this, we must look at how stars change, or evolve, throughout their lifetime. We call the study of these changes *stellar evolution.* Let us first examine how stars are born.

In the spaces between the stars there are many clouds of dust and gas. These are the *nebulae* (pl. of *nebula*); nebula is the Latin word for "cloud."

Most nebulae appear to be very thick and dense, sometimes even blocking the light of stars behind them. But actually they are very, very thin. In an average nebula there are about 1,000 particles per cubic centimeter. (A cubic centimeter is the size of a small marble.) This may seem like a lot, but not if we compare it to the air we breathe, which normally contains many *billions* of particles per cubic centimeter!

Most of the particles in a nebula are hydrogen atoms. Other gaseous elements are present, too, such as helium, oxygen, and nitrogen, but these are extremely rare compared to hydrogen. There are also some grains of dust in the nebula, but these are also much fewer in number than the gas atoms.

*The Horsehead Nebula.
This dark nebula hides the light
of the stars behind it.*

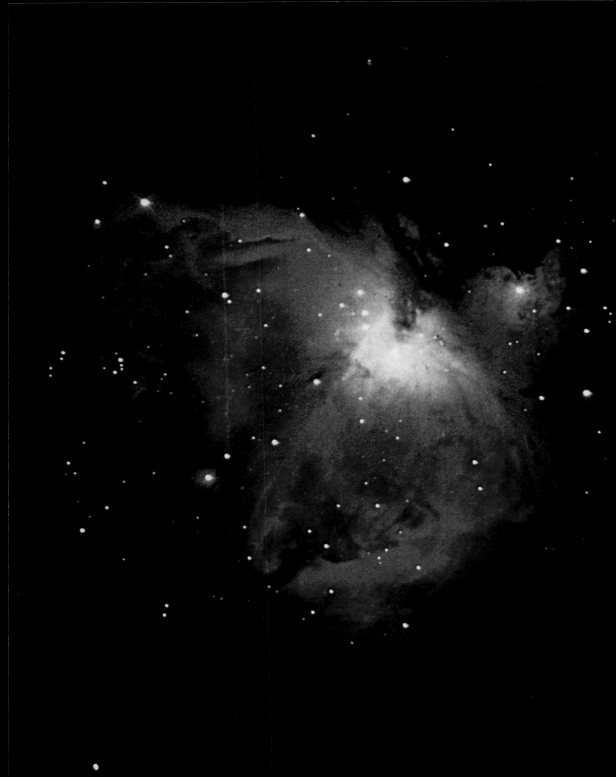

The dust particles are bigger than the gas atoms but still have diameters less than 1/1,000 of a millimeter. They are made up of minerals such as graphite, silicate, and iron.

We are able to see the nebulae because of the stars near or inside of them. The starlight shining on the gas and dust particles illuminates them, creating for us some of the most beautiful sights in the universe. One of these is the Orion Nebula in the constellation Orion, the hunter.

Within some nebulae astronomers have found dense balls of dust and gas, much denser than the rest of the matter in the nebula. These are called *globules*. The globules are slowly contracting, and it is believed that someday they will become stars.

Because stars are believed to start their existence as globules deep within the dust and gas of a nebula, these clouds have been called "stellar nurseries." In the Orion Nebula there are several globules and also four very bright stars that began shining only about 100,000 years ago. This is a very short time in astronomical terms.

There are other stars in the Orion Nebula that are still in the process of being formed. These do not shine with visible light yet, but they do radiate infrared and radio energy. Many thousands of years from now they will also "turn on." Then they will either burn off or blow away the overlying clouds that hide them at present.

The Rosette Nebula is another stellar nursery. This round, roselike beauty is found in the constellation Monoceros. In its hollow center is a cluster of very young, very bright stars.

How do globules become stars? The globules in a nebula have more gravitational attraction than the dust and gas around them. They can pull matter toward them and grow

The Orion Nebula

bigger. This increases their gravitational attraction even more. Particles of matter fall into these growing globules, called *protostars*, from greater and greater distances away.

Eventually the protostar gets so big that it starts to contract, or collapse, under its own weight. Its outer layers get so heavy that they start falling toward the center. This inward motion causes the interior regions to heat up. As we have seen, when extremely high temperatures and pressures are reached, nuclear reactions begin. The hydrogen in the core starts being converted into helium. Energy released from this reaction pushes its way outward and upward toward the surface of the protostar.

This outward pressure eventually becomes strong enough to offset the weight of the matter pushing downward, and the protostar stops contracting. It becomes stable. In its core hydrogen continues to be transformed into helium at a rate great enough to keep the star from collapsing. The energy that is produced eventually reaches the surface and is seen as starlight. The protostar is now a true star.

Some globules are able to attract much more matter than others from the surrounding nebula. These more massive globules will contract, or collapse, much faster than the smaller ones because their greater mass gives them a stronger gravitational pull on the gas and dust particles. The matter "falls in" more rapidly. The contraction from globule to star takes only a fraction of the time required for less massive bodies.

More massive stars have much heavier outer layers of gases than do smaller stars. Therefore they require more energy to remain stable. Although they also produce their energy by converting hydrogen into helium, the rate at which they do this must be greater than that of less massive stars.

The Rosette Nebula

When this additional energy reaches the star's surface, it makes it hotter and brighter. Such a star would be classified as an O-, B-, or A-type star.

Because these hot, bright stars must use up their hydrogen at a much faster rate than the cooler stars, they exhaust their fuel supply in only a few million years. The sun, on the other hand, will take about 10 billion years to use up all the hydrogen in its core. Stars with much less mass than the sun can keep "burning" hydrogen for 30 to 40 billion years. They require comparatively little energy from their core to maintain a stable condition. These are the very cool, red, M-type stars.

It may seem strange that stars with so much more hydrogen fuel than the sun should use it up more quickly. As an everyday example of this, a large car may have a bigger gas tank than a small car, but because the large car requires more fuel per mile driven, it may be out of gas long before the small car.

CHAPTER SIX

RED GIANTS, WHITE DWARFS

What happens to a star once all the hydrogen in its core has been transformed into helium? It can no longer produce energy this way. Its core starts to collapse again.

Some energy is released by this gravitational contraction of the core, enough to push the outer parts of the star farther outward. The core gets smaller and denser while the surrounding gases expand and become bloated. The star's size increases enormously.

It now has a much larger surface. The energy it emits is spread out over a greater area and is therefore not as intense as it was before. The star's surface temperature drops, and the star becomes redder in color. It has become a *red giant*. If it is one of the more massive stars, it might even become a supergiant.

With such an increase in size, although its surface temperature is quite cool, the star's luminosity can be anywhere from 100 to 10,000 times that of the sun. It has grown 10 to 500 times the solar diameter without any increase in mass.

Meanwhile, the helium core of a red giant continues to contract under its own weight, and its temperature continues to

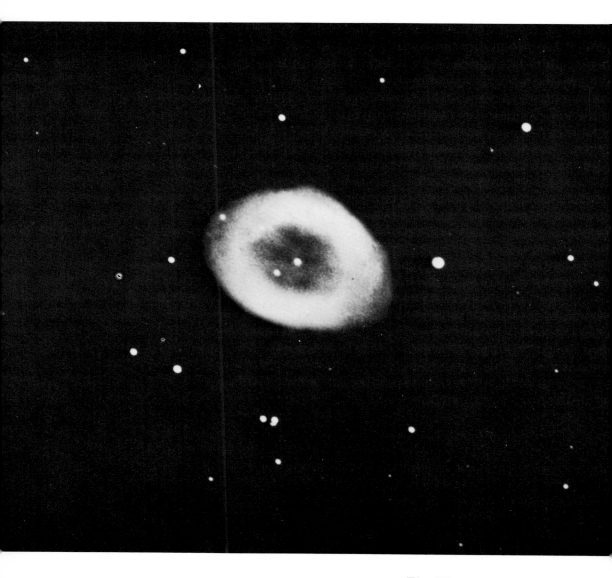

*The Ring Nebula,
a planetary nebula*

rise. When the temperature exceeds 180 million degrees F (100 million degrees C), nuclear reactions involving helium become possible. Helium begins to be converted into carbon. Energy is again released, and for a while the star is again stabilized.

Eventually, however, the helium in the core also gets used up. Once again the star begins to collapse. Its mass will determine what happens to it next.

Some stars go through an unstable period in which they keep contracting and expanding in an effort to achieve stability. These changes in size cause changes in the star's brightness. Such stars are called *variable stars* because their magnitudes keep varying.

There are other groups of evolving stars that, instead of contracting and expanding at this stage, eject large shells of their gaseous matter into space. Each shell of material may contain 10 to 20 percent of the original mass of the star. A star going through this stage is called a *planetary nebula* because through a small telescope it appears to be round and planetlike rather than a point of light, as a normal star appears. One of the most famous planetary nebulae is the Ring Nebula in the constellation Lyra.

It is believed that all stars with relatively small masses, including the sun, will eventually pass through the planetary nebula stage. These stars cannot generate nuclear reactions involving elements heavier than carbon. The shedding of its matter by the ejection of gas shells may represent the star's final death throes before it collapses into its final stage as a *white dwarf*.

The majority of stars end their existence as white dwarfs. No new energy can be created to hold up the star's outer layers. The star slowly contracts. The particles of matter draw closer and closer together, causing the stellar material to become far denser than any substance we know of here on earth. Only when the atomic particles can be squeezed no closer together does the collapse of the star stop. By this time the star is about the size of the earth but still has the mass of the sun. A golf ball of this dense material would weigh several tons here on earth.

Because the star has collapsed to such a small size, its surface is now extremely small. Its surface temperature again begins to rise dramatically because the energy it emits is concentrated in a smaller surface area. The star becomes a very small, hot, A-type star. However, because it is so small, it is also very dim. White dwarfs can be seen only with powerful telescopes.

The white dwarf now slowly cools off. Eventually it will become a burned-out black chunk of very dense matter. Because this period of cooling off is extremely long, probably longer than the age of our galaxy itself, astronomers do not believe that there are any such "black dwarfs" in our own galaxy.

In many cases white dwarfs are found to be members of a two-star, or *binary,* system. The two stars are revolving around each other in space. They are believed to have formed at the same time from the same nebula but do not necessarily have the same amount of mass. As always, the more massive star will reach its final stages first. It becomes a white dwarf while its companion star may not even have yet reached the red giant stage.

When the less massive star in the binary system does reach the red giant stage, it gets so large that some of its bloated outer layers of gas may flow onto the surface of the white dwarf. The immense gravity on the white dwarf's surface compresses these gases until a nuclear reaction occurs. Hydrogen changes into helium with a huge production of energy.

A small amount of the gaseous matter is rapidly ejected into space, and the white dwarf's luminosity suddenly increases many thousands of times. This explosion is called a *nova* because originally it was believed that the star was indeed "new"—that it had just been created. Such a concept is understandable, since before the eruption no star had usually been seen in that location of the sky.

The white dwarf soon returns to its former quiet and dim state, but it may go nova again if its surface is disturbed by more matter flowing onto it from its companion star. Although we cannot see all the novae—even at their brightest—because of their great distances from us, it is estimated that several dozen such explosions occur in our own galaxy every year.

CHAPTER SEVEN

THE FINAL STAGES

Up until now we have been talking about stars whose masses are equal to or less than that of the sun. With these stars, once the helium in the core has been converted into carbon, the mass of the star is not great enough to set in motion further nuclear reactions. And so they collapse into white dwarfs.

But what about the more massive star? What happens to it? The larger star evolves much more rapidly and reaches the red giant stage very quickly. As with smaller stars, the core becomes mainly carbon and starts to contract. But because of the large star's greater mass, this contraction produces the extreme temperatures and pressures needed for nuclear reactions involving the carbon. The star now uses the carbon as its fuel and produces enough energy to once again stop the contraction of its core. It converts the carbon into a heavier element.

This process is repeated many times, as heavier and heavier elements are created in the core. Many of the chemical elements we know to exist in the universe are believed to have been created in the cores of these massive supergiant stars.

There comes a point, however, when the star finally loses its ability to create any more nuclear energy. The core can no longer withstand the tremendous weight of the overlying layers, and it collapses. But it does not contract slowly, like a white dwarf. Instead, it collapses very suddenly. This implosion (inward explosion) causes a tremendous explosion in the outer layers of the star. Gaseous material is hurled out into space at speeds of over 3,000 miles (4,800 km) per second. It is these hot gases that we see as a *supernova.*

Although a nova and a supernova have similar names and are both stellar explosions, they are very different events. They differ both in the cause and size of the explosion. They are like the difference between a small firecracker and a stick of dynamite. Only a small percentage of the white dwarf star is blown into space in a nova explosion, whereas a major portion of the supernova star is blown away. The supernova star flares up to many millions of times brighter than its original state, and for several weeks it may even shine more brightly than the entire galaxy in which it is located.

At most, supernovae only occur once or twice a century in any one galaxy, and they fade after only a few months to a year. But the gases that have been hurled into space continue to be visible (through a telescope) for many centuries. These are called *supernova remnants.*

The most famous supernova remnant is the Crab Nebula in the constellation Taurus. It was created from a supernova explosion that was seen and recorded by Chinese astronomers in A.D. 1054. The gases are still rushing away into space. The Veil Nebula in the constellation Cygnus is another supernova remnant. It is much older than the Crab Nebula.

Even after a supernova explosion, a small portion of the original star is left. This is the core, which has collapsed because it can no longer produce enough energy to withstand the weight of its outer layers. Its collapse is like the crumbling of a tall building when the foundation gives way.

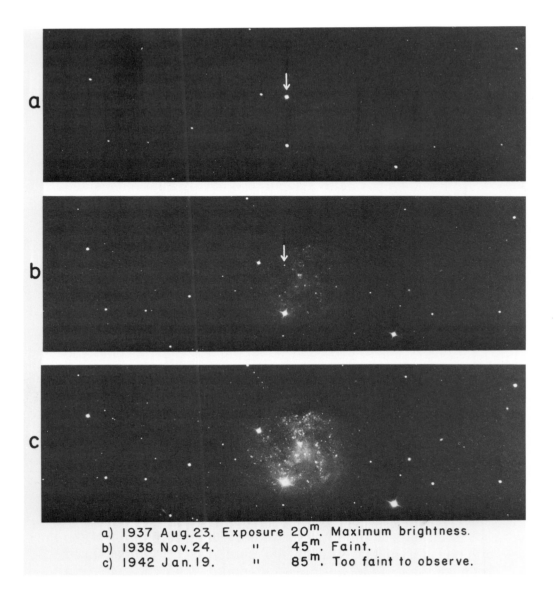

a) 1937 Aug. 23. Exposure 20^m. Maximum brightness.
b) 1938 Nov. 24.   "   45^m. Faint.
c) 1942 Jan. 19.   "   85^m. Too faint to observe.

A supernova in IC 4182, a distant galaxy

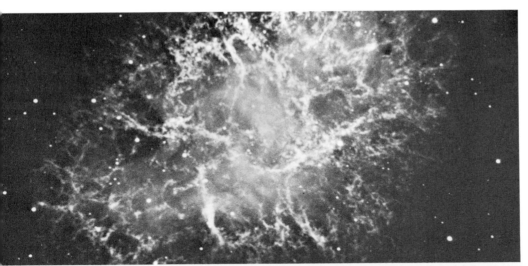

Above: *the Crab Nebula, a supernova remnant.*
Below: *a portion of the Veil Nebula,*
also a supernova remnant

In the sudden collapse of the core, the atomic particles are not just pushed closer together as they are in the white dwarf. They are actually forced to combine with each other. The tremendous impact of the implosion pushes the electrons, which are negatively charged, into the atomic nuclei. These nuclei normally consist only of protons, which are positively charged, and neutrons, which have no charge. The electrons and protons combine to form more neutrons. Thus, the stellar material comes to consist of neutrons only. Once the neutrons are pushed very close together, the star's collapse is halted. A *neutron star* has been formed.

A neutron star is much denser than a white dwarf. A cubic centimeter of a neutron star's material would weigh a billion tons on earth. And whereas a white dwarf collapses only to about the size of the earth, a neutron star gets as small as 9 to 12 miles (14.4 to 19.2 km) in diameter.

Astronomers discovered neutron stars by the very precise and rapid bursts of energy they emit. These "pulses" occur many times every second. Until astronomers had instruments precise enough to detect these rapid flashes, they thought they were seeing ordinary stars. Even after the so-called *pulsars* ("pulsing stars") were discovered, it was not known what caused them to emit energy the way they did. And no one knew what kind of star they were.

Then one was discovered in the middle of the Crab Nebula that fit the model astronomers had previously calculated for a neutron star. It was realized that the mysterious pulsars were neutron stars, created by supernovae explosions.

The rapid collapse of the neutron star causes it to start spinning very rapidly. "Hot spots" on its surface emit intense amounts of energy. Like a lighthouse beam, every time such a hot spot whirls around to our direction, we detect it as a pulse.

The neutron star is the second possible path that an aging star can take in its final stages. Only stars that are several times more massive than our sun can ever evolve into such stars. But what happens to those stars that are 10 or 20 times more massive?

As we have seen, a white dwarf is about as massive as our sun but has shrunk to about the size of the earth. A neutron star may have two or three times the mass of the sun but has become even smaller than the earth. In each case, powerful forces have managed to stop the gravitational contraction of the star at some point.

Some stars have far more mass than those that become neutron stars. Because such a star is so much more massive, the resulting collapse is that much greater. In fact, there is no force in the universe strong enough to stop it. The matter in the core is squeezed and squeezed by the pressure of the overlying layers of gaseous material until it is theoretically crushed out of existence. All that is believed to be left is its gravitational field, which grows stronger and stronger as the star becomes more and more compact.

The star's gravitational field eventually gets so strong that nothing in the area can escape it. Every particle of matter or quantum of energy that comes close to such a star is pulled into it and can never leave. Light itself cannot escape the star. Therefore, we cannot see it. The star has become a *black hole.*

Although astronomers have not yet positively identified any black holes, they are strongly convinced they have located several, each of which is a member of a binary-star system. One is called Cygnus X-1, found in the constellation Cygnus. (The X-1 designation refers to the fact that this was the first X-ray source discovered in the constellation Cygnus.) The visible star of this binary is a hot, blue supergiant with about 30 times the mass of the sun. Circling this massive star is an unseen companion of about 10 solar masses. It is this unseen object that is believed to be a black hole. As the two stars orbit each other, the black hole attracts gases away from its companion. The gases swirl into the hole and become so hot that they generate intense X rays that have been detected by astronomers.

During the last stages of any star's existence, many changes take place. Regardless of its mass, the star throws part of itself off into space. Such eruptions may be very peaceful, like the planetary nebula's expanding shells, or very violent, like a supernova. A small percentage of this material is no longer simply hydrogen or helium but has already been transformed into heavier elements. All of this matter—the hydrogen, helium, and heavier elements—may eventually be included in the dust and gas clouds, the nebulae, that in time will become new stars and possibly even new solar systems. These new stars will have greater amounts of heavier elements than the stars that formed earlier.

Our sun is one of these newer stars. The entire solar system was formed from the same nebula that formed the sun. The carbon, oxygen, iron, and other elements we find here on earth were probably created in the interior of some aged star before it erupted and sent its matter out into space.

CHAPTER EIGHT

STAR GROUPS

Although the sun is an average star in luminosity, size, and temperature, it is unusual in one way. It is a single star. It does not have any companion stars around it. This is true of only about 15 percent of all stars. The rest are in multiple-star systems, most of which are made up of only two stars. In a binary, the two stars are revolving around each other in space.

Most binaries look like single stars to the naked eye. A telescope is usually needed to see the stars as separate bodies. However, one famous binary was known to the ancient Arabs centuries before the invention of the telescope. This is the middle star in the handle of the Big Dipper. If you have very good eyesight, on a clear night you should be able to see the two stars in this location without a telescope. They are called Mizar and Alcor. Legend has it that the ancient Arabs used this pair of stars as an eye test.

Although about half of all stars are members of binaries, there are many other multiple-star systems. There can be 3, 4, 12, or many more stars in such a group, all held together by their mutual gravitational attraction. They all move together through space like a flock of geese. It is believed that all the stars in such a group were formed at the same time.

Why did some stars form into binaries or larger star groups while others, like our sun, evolved alone? We do not know. Nor do we know if there are other planetary systems like our solar system. Planets are relatively small bodies and shine only by the reflected light of their star. From distances such as those that exist between stars, a planet's dim light is lost in the glare of the star. However, astronomers generally believe that many single stars, like our sun, do have planetary systems similar to our own. Most of them think that stars evolve either as part of a multiple-star system or as a single star with planets.

Larger star groups are called *star clusters.* They may have hundreds or even thousands of member stars. The most common type of star cluster is the *open cluster;* the Pleiades and Hyades are examples of this. Hundreds of open clusters have been found in our galaxy. As the name implies, open clusters are loosely formed, with no special distinguishing shape. Each contains several hundred stars, most of which are visible only through powerful telescopes. The stars in an open cluster are relatively young stars. Some astronomers believe that open-cluster stars eventually separate from each other and become single-, double-, or multiple-star systems. If this is true, it is possible that our sun was once a member of such a cluster.

There is another type of star cluster that is very different from the open cluster. This is the *globular cluster.* Only about 125 globular clusters have been found in our own galaxy, but many more than this are known to exist in other galaxies.

Above: *the Pleiades,*
an open star cluster.
Below: *a globular cluster*

The stars in a globular cluster are relatively closely packed into a spherical shape some 100 light-years across. There may be many thousands of stars in one of these clusters. Globular cluster stars are very old. These clusters stay together throughout their lifetime.

Any star cluster bigger than a globular cluster would have to be considered a galaxy in its own right. In fact, if a globular cluster were found alone in space, it would be defined as a very small galaxy. Usually, however, they are found around the center of a galaxy.

But what exactly is a galaxy? It is the largest kind of star system there is. Our sun is a member of such a star system along with perhaps a hundred billion other stars. The name of our galaxy is the *Milky Way.*

All of the stars in the Milky Way, including the sun, revolve around the center of the galaxy, each at its own rate. The sun, for example, moves at 150 miles (240 km) per second relative to the center, but the galaxy is so big that it takes approximately 200 million years for the sun to make one complete revolution. Of course, the solar system, including the earth, moves with the sun. We call each revolution a *galactic year.*

Astronomers estimate that there are perhaps a billion other galaxies scattered throughout the visible universe. Although not all galaxies have the same number of stars in them, you can get some idea of how many billions of stars there are in the universe. Do you know how big a billion of anything is? You will not have lived one billion seconds until you are about 32 years old!

The Andromeda Galaxy is named after the constellation in which it appears. It is one of the very few galaxies that can be seen from the earth without a telescope. But it is so very far away that even when we use the most powerful telescopes we are able to distinguish only the very brightest stars in it. The Andromeda Galaxy is more than 2 million light-years away. The light we see coming from it has been traveling through space for over 2 million years.

The Andromeda Galaxy

The Milky Way band of stars in the sky

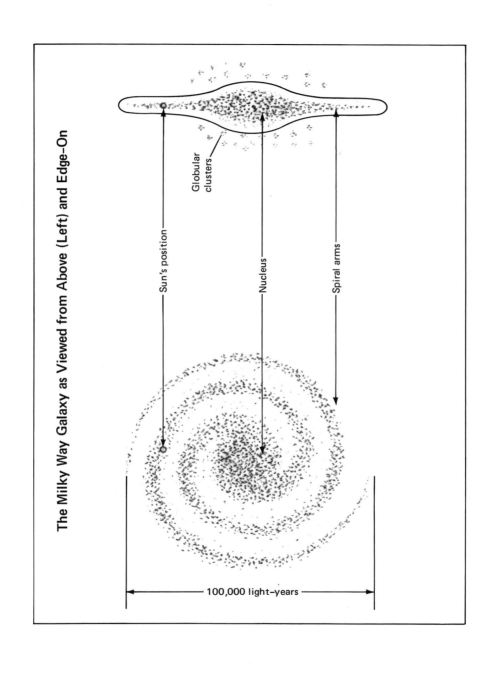

The Milky Way Galaxy as Viewed from Above (Left) and Edge-On

Sun's position

Globular clusters

Nucleus

Spiral arms

100,000 light-years

In the photograph of the Andromeda Galaxy the white points of light surrounding it are stars from our own galaxy, the Milky Way. We are looking "through" them to the much more distant galaxy beyond. It is like looking through a paint-spattered window to a scene outside.

Astronomers believe that the Milky Way looks very much like the Andromeda Galaxy. As you can see from the diagram, if we could get outside the Milky Way and view it from above, it would look like a giant pinwheel, with its long arms of stars spiraling out from its center, or *nucleus.* For this reason, the Milky Way is called a *spiral galaxy.* The Andromeda Galaxy is also a spiral galaxy. Globular clusters form a sort of halo around the nucleus of both galaxies.

Viewed from the side, the Milky Way looks like two Frisbees stuck together. The "plane" of the galaxy is where the Frisbees' rims touch. Note that the sun (and the solar system) is located along this plane but way out near the edge of the galaxy, not near the center. Most of the nebulae and open-star clusters are also found along the galactic plane.

Because of our location in the Milky Way, when we look from the earth in a direction away from the plane of our galaxy, we see few stars. We are looking along the thinnest part of the galaxy, viewing it edge-on. But when we look along the plane, the number of stars becomes so great that all we see with the naked eye is a faint, whitish, rather ragged band cutting across the entire sky.

This band of light is what some ancient peoples called the "pathway of the gods," or the "Milky Way." Even Columbus and the other early explorers had no idea that the "milky" path in the sky was actually many hundreds of stars very close together in the sky. We must be careful to distinguish between this white band that we see in the sky and the galaxy itself. Both have the same name, but they are not the same thing. With a small telescope or a good pair of binoculars, you can see separate stars in the "Milky Way" area of the sky.

CHAPTER NINE

GALAXIES

There are a billion galaxies, and each has hundreds of billions of stars. Each of these stars is at a particular stage in its own individual evolution. Although we have been describing the stars in our own galaxy—the Milky Way—because we can study them more closely, the stars in other galaxies are very similar. Between the stars, particularly along the plane of the spiral galaxies, there are dust and gas particles that make up the nebulae.

No two galaxies are exactly the same, but galaxies can generally be grouped into three basic types. The Milky Way and the Andromeda Galaxy are called *spiral galaxies* because of their spiral arms and pinwheel shapes. However, other spiral galaxies may appear to be different. For example, the spiral arms can be very tightly wound, as in the Andromeda Galaxy, or they may be more open, as in the spiral galaxy in Ursa Major. The size of the nucleus sometimes dominates the appearance of a galaxy, while in others it is very small and compact in relation to the arms.

Some spiral galaxies have bars of stars and dust running through their centers. Their spiral arms start at the ends of these bars and again can be either tightly or loosely wound around the nucleus. Not surprisingly, these galaxies are called *barred spirals.*

Spiral galaxies range in size from about 20,000 light-years to more than 100,000 light-years in diameter. The Milky Way and Andromeda are two of the larger spirals. But even the smaller ones have at least one billion stars in them, and many have a lot more.

A second type of galaxy is called an *elliptical galaxy.* Elliptical galaxies look somewhat like spiral galaxies, but they don't have any arms. Some are round in shape while others are oval.

There are more elliptical galaxies than spirals, but most ellipticals are very small and dim and therefore cannot be seen at great distances. For this reason, spirals represent more than two thirds of the thousand brightest galaxies in the sky.

The small dwarf ellipticals, the most common type of galaxy, can be as small as 5,000 light-years in diameter. That's not much bigger than the globular clusters that we find surrounding the nucleus of our own galaxy.

At the other extreme, however, there are giant ellipticals with 10 times the luminosity of the Andromeda Galaxy. These giants are several hundred thousand light-years in diameter, with 100 times more stars than are in the Milky Way.

The third type of galaxy is called an *irregular galaxy.* It has no definite shape and doesn't look like either a spiral or an elliptical galaxy. Some irregular galaxies may have their odd shape because of a collision with another galaxy. Others are distorted by the gravitational effects of nearby galaxies. Two such irregular galaxies are small satellites of the Milky Way.

Above: *a spiral galaxy in the constellation Ursa Major.*
Below: *a barred spiral galaxy.*

—52

They are called the Large and Small Magellanic Clouds, and they can be seen on earth only from the southern hemisphere. They were named for the famous explorer Magellan, who sighted them on his round-the-world voyage.

Like the whitish band in the sky which we call the Milky Way, the Magellanic Clouds also appear as large white fuzzy patches in the sky. That is why they were called "clouds," although even the astronomers of Magellan's day knew that they were not clouds like those in the earth's atmosphere. It should also be remembered that Magellan was not the first to discover these celestial objects. They were well known to the many tribes that lived south of the equator long before Magellan and his crew ever sighted them.

Astronomers do not know why one galaxy developed spiral arms or a bar through its nucleus and why another became oval or round in shape. They do know, however, that the galaxies are not spread evenly over the billions of light-years of space in the visible universe but rather are grouped into clusters held together by gravity.

Our galaxy, the Milky Way, is a member of a small cluster of galaxies called the *Local Group,* which has around two dozen members spread over a region of about 3 million light-years in diameter. The Milky Way and the Andromeda Galaxy are the biggest galaxies in this cluster.

The Local Group is a relatively small cluster. Others, such as the Virgo cluster, have thousands of members. As with some of the galaxies, the clusters are named after the constellation in which they appear.

There are several clusters of galaxies less than 250 million light-years away. These are close enough for us to distinguish the features of individual members. But beyond these relatively

The Large Magellanic Cloud

nearby clusters lie many large ones that, because they are so distant, appear much more compact. Their individual galaxies look almost like stars clustered together. However, these galaxies are as far apart from each other as are the galaxies in the Local Group or other clusters nearer to us.

Some astronomers believe that there is evidence that nearby clusters of galaxies form a "supergalaxy." There are around 65 such clusters within about 50 million light-years of the Local Group. Most of these lie on or near the same plane, similar to the way most of the stars in the Milky Way lie on or near the galactic plane. If such a supergalaxy exists, it would have a diameter of some 100 to 200 million light-years, and its center would probably lie in the direction of the constellation Virgo, where the Virgo cluster is. There is also some evidence that clusters of galaxies beyond this local supergalaxy may also be grouped into supergalaxies.

Beyond most of the galaxies and clusters of galaxies that can be detected, astronomers have found the *quasars* (for "quasi-stellar radio sources"). In a telescope these mysterious objects look like stars but they continuously emit enormous amounts of energy, far more than the average star. In fact, they may be giving off more than 100 times the total energy of all the stars in the Milky Way. But they are very small objects, only about one light-year in diameter.

We don't know exactly what the quasars are, but we do know that the energy we receive from them started out billions of years ago in its journey toward us. We see the quasars today as they were then, when that light left them, not as they may be today. It is thought that perhaps they are the extremely bright centers of very young developing galaxies. There aren't any quasars near us now, but perhaps the Milky Way was quasar-like in its early stages also. If the light from the newborn Milky Way left here billions of years ago, perhaps some astronomer in a very distant galaxy is now seeing that light and therefore seeing us as a quasar.

CHAPTER TEN

THE EXPANDING UNIVERSE

People long ago believed that the earth was the center of the universe. It was thought to be a stationary object, with all the stars, planets, and even the sun revolving around it.

When it was discovered that the earth actually revolves around the sun and is therefore not motionless, it was believed that the sun was the center of the universe and did not move. This universe was thought to consist of only one galaxy, the Milky Way. Only 65 years ago astronomers were convinced that nothing existed beyond the limits of that galaxy. The Milky Way was an island universe floating in an enormous sea of empty space.

Only after other island universes, or galaxies, were found to lie outside the Milky Way did astronomers begin to realize how very big the universe really is. And then another startling discovery was made. The universe, far from being a static thing, was expanding! All of the galaxies were found to be moving farther and farther away from each other! The ones farthest from us are moving away at greater speeds than those close by. This would be true no matter where in the universe we were, because we are not at the center of the universe.

There is no center, just as there is no "center" on the surface of the earth.

From where we are in the universe, the Virgo cluster of galaxies is moving away from us at a speed of 750 miles (1,200 km) per second. It is about 80 million light-years away. The Corona Borealis cluster of galaxies, which is 1.4 billion light-years away, is moving away from us at 13,400 miles (21,440 km) per second. Many of the quasars, which are the most distant objects known, are receding at velocities more than one half the speed of light.

Put some ink dots on a round balloon, then blow the balloon up. Nearby dots will separate only an inch (2.5 cm) or so, whereas dots farther apart may end up with 2 or 3 inches (5 to 7.5 cm) between them. Since the dots all separated in the same amount of time (the time it took you to blow up the balloon), those that are 2 or 3 inches apart had to have separated at a faster rate to have covered the greater distance. Note that none of the dots can be considered to be at the center of the balloon.

If all the clusters of galaxies are speeding away from each other, and if this speed was maintained throughout history, was there a time when everything was clumped together? If so, how long ago was everything back at the starting point? And what was that starting point?

Astronomers have calculated that approximately 13 to 18 billion years ago all the matter and energy in the universe was concentrated in a single, small, unstructured primordial mass. None of the galaxies, stars, or planets had been formed yet. A violent explosion of this mass of matter and energy started the expansion or movement of everything outward. This explosion is called the *Big Bang.*

There is much evidence to support the Big Bang theory. It is the one generally accepted by most scientists to explain the origin of the universe. An enormous amount of energy was released in this explosion. Recently scientists have detected this energy, now in a much weaker form, still moving through the universe.

The big question today is whether the universe will go on expanding forever, as it has been doing for 18 billion years or so, or whether the expansion will slow down and the universe will start to contract back in upon itself. The course it takes depends upon how much matter, or mass, there is in the universe. It is this matter that has the gravitational force to stop the expansion. As big and as numerous as the galaxies are, astronomers have not yet been able to come up with the amount of matter they believe is needed to slow down the expanding universe.

However, recent studies may have found a previously unknown amount of mass in the form of one of the most abundant yet smallest particles of matter. These particles are called *neutrinos.* If neutrinos do, in fact, have the mass that some scientists believe they do, it will be enough to slow the expansion of the universe and eventually cause it to contract again. If this happens, once the universe is again a primordial mass, it may explode once more, and the expansion will start all over again. A new universe will be created. Scientists call this the *Oscillating Universe* theory.

How fortunate we are to be living at a time when so many discoveries are being made! Our knowledge of the universe grows with every passing day. How different are the ideas of today from those of only a few dozen years ago! What lies ahead should be even more exciting.

THE CONSTELLATIONS

Name	Description
Andromeda	Princess
Antlia	Air Pump
Apus	Bird of Paradise
Aquarius	Water Bearer
Aquila	Eagle
Ara	Altar
Aries	Ram
Auriga	Charioteer
Boötes	Herdsman
Caelum	Chisel
Camelopardalus	Giraffe
Cancer	Crab
Canes Venatici	Hunting dogs
Canis Major	Big Dog
Canis Minor	Little Dog
Capricornus	Sea Goat
Carina	Keel of Ship
Cassiopeia	Queen
Centaurus	Centaur
Cepheus	King
Cetus	Whale
Chamaeleon	Chameleon
Circinus	Compasses
Columba	Dove
Coma Berenices	Berenice's Hair
Corona Australis	Southern Crown
Corona Borealis	Northern Crown
Corvus	Crow
Crater	Cup
Crux	Southern Cross

Name	Description
Cygnus	Swan
Delphinus	Dolphin
Dorado	Swordfish
Draco	Dragon
Equuleus	Little Horse
Eridanus	River
Fornax	Furnace
Gemini	Twins
Grus	Crane
Hercules	Son of Zeus
Horologium	Clock
Hydra	Sea Serpent
Hydrus	Water Snake
Indus	Indian
Lacerta	Lizard
Leo	Lion
Leo Minor	Little Lion
Lepus	Hare
Libra	Scales
Lupus	Wolf
Lynx	Lynx
Lyra	Lyre
Mensa	Table Mountain
Microscopium	Microscope
Monoceros	Unicorn
Musca	Fly
Norma	Octant
Octans	Carpenter's Level
Ophiuchus	Serpent Bearer
Orion	Hunter

Name	Description
Pavo	Peacock
Pegasus	Winged Horse
Perseus	The Hero Perseus
Phoenix	Phoenix
Pictor	Easel
Pisces	Fish
Piscis Austrinus	Southern Fish
Puppis	Stern of Ship
Pyxis (Malus)	Compass on Ship
Reticulum	Net
Sagitta	Arrow
Sagittarius	Archer
Scorpius	Scorpion
Sculptor	Sculptor's Tools
Scutum	Shield
Serpens	Serpent
Sextans	Sextant
Taurus	Bull
Telescopium	Telescope
Triangulum	Triangle
Triangulum Australe	Southern Triangle
Tucana	Toucan
Ursa Major	Big Bear**
Ursa Minor	Little Bear**
Vela	Sail of Ship
Virgo	Virgin
Volans	Flying fish
Vulpecula	Little Fox

**The "Big Dipper" is part of Ursa Major; the "Little Dipper" is part of Ursa Minor.

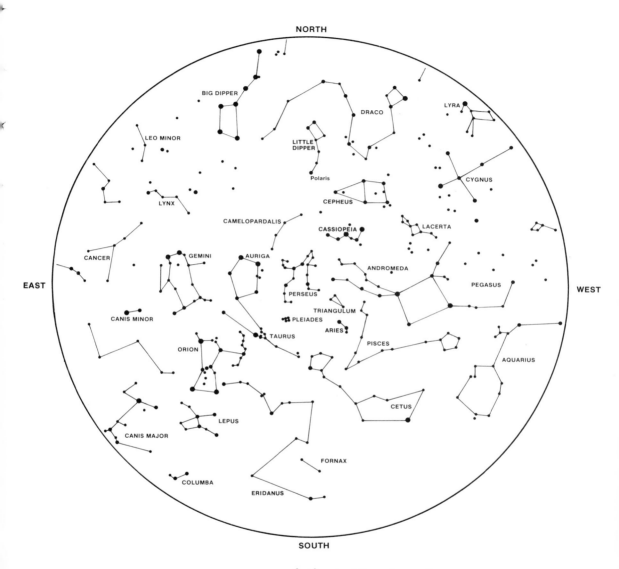

A chart of the sky as it appears every December at approximately 10:30 P.M.

THE NEAREST STARS

Star	Magnitude Abs.	Magnitude App.	Distance (l.y.)	Spectral Class
1 Sun	4.8	—26.8	**	G2
2 α Centauri***	4.4	0.1	4.3	G2
3 Barnard's Star	13.2	9.5	5.9	M5
4 Wolf 359	16.8	13.5	7.6	M6
5 Lalande 21185	10.5	7.5	8.1	M2
6 Sirius***	1.4	—1.5	8.6	A1
7 Luyten 726-8***	15.4	12.5	8.9	M6
8 Ross 154	13.3	10.6	9.4	M5
9 Ross 248	14.7	12.2	10.3	M6
10 ε Eridani	6.1	3.7	10.7	K2
11 Luyten 789-6	14.9	12.2	10.8	M6
12 Ross 128	13.5	11.1	10.8	M5
13 61 Cygni***	7.5	5.2	11.2	K5
14 ε Indi	7.0	4.7	11.2	K5
15 Procyon***	2.7	0.3	11.4	F5
16 Σ2398***	11.1	8.9	11.5	M3.5
17 BD +43°44	10.3	8.1	11.6	M1
18 CD —36°15693	9.6	7.4	11.7	M2
19 τ Ceti	5.7	3.5	11.9	G8
20 BD +5° 1668	11.9	9.8	12.2	M4
21 CD —39° 14192	8.7	6.7	12.5	M1
22 Kapteyn's Star	10.8	8.8	12.7	M0
23 Kruger 60***	11.8	9.7	12.8	M4
24 Ross 614***	13.1	11.3	13.1	M5
25 BD —12° 4523	12.0	10.0	13.1	M5

**8 light-minutes.
***Star is a multiple-star system. Magnitude and spectral class
  are given only for the major star in the system.

THE BRIGHTEST STARS

Star		Common Name	Magnitude App.	Abs.	Dist. (l.y.)	Spectral Class	Size
1	Sun		−26.8	+4.8	**	G2	
2	α Canis Majoris**	Sirius	−1.42	+1.4	8.7	A1	
3	α Carinae	Canopus	−0.72	−3.1	98	F0	Supergiant
4	α Boötis	Arcturus	−0.06	−0.3	36	K2	Giant
5	α Centauri***		−0.02	+4.4	4.3	G2	
6	α Lyrae	Vega	0.04	+0.5	26.5	A0	
7	α Aurigae	Capella	0.05	−0.6	45	G2	Giant
8	β Orionis***	Rigel	0.14	−7.1	900	B8	Supergiant
9	α Canis Minoris	Procyon	0.37	+2.7	11.3	F5	
10	α Orionis	Betelgeuse	0.41	−5.6	520	M2	Supergiant
11	α Eridani	Achernar	0.51	−2.3	118	B5	
12	β Centauri	Hadar	0.63	−5.2	490	B1	Giant
13	α Aquilae	Altair	0.77	+2.2	16.5	A7	
14	α Tauri***	Aldebaran	0.86	−0.7	68	K5	Giant
15	α Virginis	Spica	0.91	−3.2	261	B1	
16	α Scorpii***	Antares	0.92	−5.1	520	M1	Supergiant
17	β Geminorum	Pollux	1.16	+1.0	35	K0	Giant
18	α Piscis Austrinus	Formalhaut	1.19	+2.0	22.6	A3	
19	α Cygni	Deneb	1.26	−7.1	1600	A2	Supergiant
20	β Crucis		1.28	−4.6	490	B0	Giant
21	α Crucis***	Acrux	1.34	−3.9	370	B1	
22	α Leonis***	Regulus	1.36	−0.7	84	B7	
23	ε Canis Majoris***	Adhara	1.48	−5.1	680	B2	Supergiant
24	λ Scorpii	Shaula	1.60	−3.3	310	B1	
25	τ Orionis	Bellatrix	1.64	−4.2	470	B2	Giant

Stars are listed in order of apparent magnitude.   **8 light-minutes.

***Star is a multiple-star system. Magnitude and spectral class
refer to the major star in the system.

GLOSSARY

Absolute magnitude—a measure of how bright a celestial object would appear on earth if it were 32.6 light-years from the earth.

Apparent magnitude—a measure of how bright a celestial object appears to an observer.

Barred spiral—a spiral galaxy in which the spiral arms start at the ends of a barlike structure passing through the nucleus of the galaxy.

Big Bang—a theory that states that the universe began with a violent explosion of a primordial mass.

Binary, or binary star—a two-star system; the two stars revolve around each other.

Black hole—a star whose matter is so dense and compacted that its gravitational field prevents all matter or energy from escaping from it.

Constellation—a group of stars that are in the same part of the sky and appear to form a pattern or picture.

Elliptical galaxy—a round or oval-shaped galaxy without any spiral arms.

Galactic year—the period of time it takes the sun to revolve around the center of the galaxy.

Galaxy—a large system of billions of stars, dust, and gas isolated in space from similar systems.

Giant—a star of large size and luminosity that has already consumed most of the hydrogen in its core; usually red in color.

Globular cluster—a compact, spherical star system containing many thousands of stars.

Globule—a very small, dark cloud of dust and gas in a nebula whose matter is thicker (denser) than the rest of the nebula.

Irregular galaxy—a galaxy that has neither a spiral nor an elliptical shape and is not symmetrical.

Light-year—the distance that light travels in one year, approximately 6 trillion miles (9,600 billion km).

Local Group—the cluster of galaxies that our own galaxy, the Milky Way, is in.

Magnitude—a measure of brightness of a celestial object.

Milky Way—the faint, ragged band of light that cuts across the sky, actually composed of many thousands of stars; the name given to our galaxy.

Nebula—an immense cloud of interstellar dust and gas.

Neutrino—a very small subatomic particle, believed to have very little or no mass and no electric charge.

Neutron star—a star of extremely high density, composed almost entirely of neutrons.

Nova—a star that greatly increases its brightness in an explosive manner.

Nuclear reaction—a change in atomic structure, causing one element to be converted into another.

Nucleus (of a galaxy)—the central portion of a galaxy; plural is *nuclei*.

Open cluster—a loose group of stars, usually from a few dozen to several hundred, moving together through the galaxy.

Oscillating Universe—a theory that states that the universe alternately expands and contracts.

Parallax, or parallactic shift—the apparent shift of an object against the background when viewed from two different positions.

Planetary nebula—a star with a shell-like atmosphere of expanding gas; not related to planets in any way.

Pulsar—a rapidly rotating neutron star.

Quasar—a celestial object with an energy output greater than that of a galaxy yet smaller in size than the average galaxy.

Red giant—see *giant*.

Spectral lines—individual lines in a spectrum, caused by the emission or absorption of energy by atoms of specific elements.

Spectrogram—the photograph of a spectrum.

Spectrograph—the instrument used to photograph a spectrum, usually attached to a telescope.

Spectrum—the array of wavelengths or colors when white light is dispersed; plural is *spectra*.

Spiral galaxy—a pinwheel-shaped galaxy with "arms" spiraling away from the nucleus.

Star cluster—a group of stars within a galaxy.

Stellar evolution—the changes that a star goes through during its existence.

Supergalaxy—a group of many clusters of galaxies.

Supergiant—an enormous star, possibly larger than the orbit of the planet Mars.

Supernova—an enormous stellar explosion that blows the star apart.

Supernova remnant—the nebula that remains after a supernova explosion.

Variable star—a star whose brightness and size changes periodically.

White dwarf—a small star in the last stages of evolution; it has collapsed to about the size of the earth but still has the mass of the sun.

White light—the combination of all the wavelengths of visible radiation.

FOR FURTHER READING

Asimov, Isaac. *Alpha Centauri, the Nearest Star.* Lothrop, Lee & Shepard: New York, 1976.

Bergamini, David. *The Universe.* Silver Burdett Co.: Morristown, N.J., 1977.

Fisher, David E. *The Creation of Atoms and Stars.* Holt, Rinehart & Winston: New York, 1979.

Gallant, Roy A. *Fires in the Sky.* Four Winds Press: New York, 1978.

Moore, Patrick. *Your Book of Astronomy.* 4th ed. (Young Readers Library) Lawrence, Mass.: Faber & Faber, 1979.

Rey, H. A. *The Stars.* Houghton Mifflin Co.: Boston, 1967 (Excellent for learning the constellations).

Also, you might consider subscribing to a magazine. *Odyssey* is an excellent astronomy magazine for younger readers. *Astronomy,* also an excellent magazine, is beautifully illustrated. Both can be ordered from 625 E. St. Paul Ave., P.O. Box 92788, Milwaukee, Wisconsin 53202.

INDEX